100

commandments to my daughter Larin

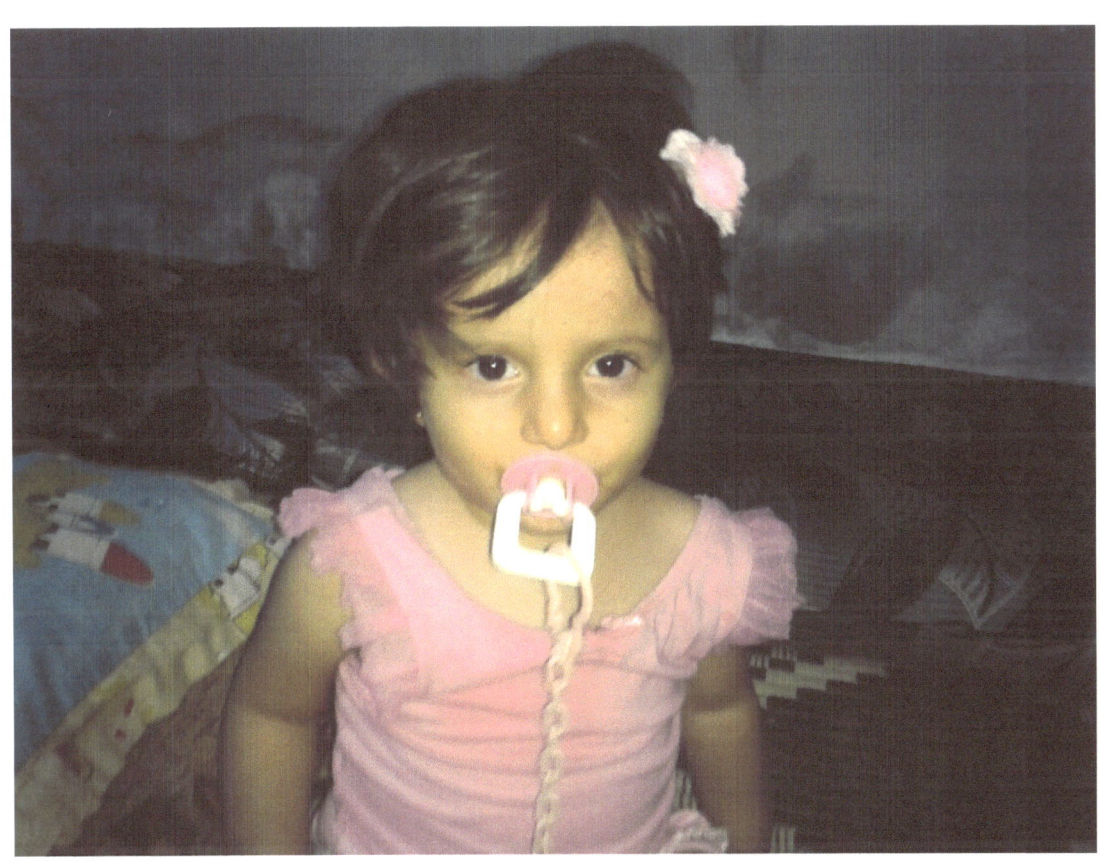

By Mustafa Kayyali

100   commandments to my daughter Larin
Copyright 2016© by Mustafa Kayyali

100   commandments to my daughter Larin

Few advices and principles for life dictated for my daughter Larin

100   commandments to my daughter Larin

Topics and roles for life to be studied and observed by my daughter Larin.

About the writer

Writer, novelist, translator, and lecturer at Idleb University, Syria. . I have wrote and translated many books in both Arabic and English. Nowadays, I am living with my wife and two daughters in Idleb, Syria.

Dedication…

I dedicate this book to my daughter Larin Kayyali.

Wish you a great peaceful life full of love and wisdom.

My daughter Larin..

It has been one year and a half since you came to this world.. since your fascinating coming illuminated my world and lightened the dark in my heart.. Here are my commandments my little angel.. take them from me.. they are the commandments of a friend to his girlfriend.. I have no pleasure in this life my girl except for your pleasure.. my ultimate goal is to see you a successful person in this community.

Now, in this moment, I can look at you while you are playing and laughing.. while you are eating and sleeping.. while you are smiling and acting in a naughty way. You are my sweet little angel.. you are my queen my little babe. Please take these commandments in the heart of yours because you are going to need them whenever you grow up.. Remember my little girl.. you are my girlfriend. Never be afraid of me because no friend be afraid from his portrait in the face of his true friend.

One day my girl.. one day, you are going to read these commandments. I do not know hence, whether we would be together, or that each one is living separately..

100 commandments to my daughter Larin

By Mustafa Kayyali

1- Do not be afraid of Truth, and never be afraid of saying the truth or passing the path of the justice even if the number of those who follow that way are few. Whatever this road become long and thorny, you would find the lifeline at its end.

2- Never show respect to anybody by kissing his hand whatever is the goal or the reason. Do not bow for anybody. Never kiss my hand or the hand of your mother as showing us respect and love, obedience or satisfaction. I so much hate this act my little angel. Never be subordinate to anybody my girl.

3- Be yourself, and never subordinate to anybody. Have your *own* independent character and never be under the objection of anyone.

4- Forget everything connected with liberation of women.. forget all slogans and mottos that calls for preserving and defending of the women. They are all banal slogans. Have in your mind subliminal goals and plans like liberation of human being in general and liberation of his mind and his thought from fear, anxiety and doubt. You have a great message and your message is dictated to the whole humanity and not to women away from the others. Never be simple minded to follow such trifle mottos.

5- Whenever you have the chance to travel, do that without hesitation. If you could not have the chance to travel, then let your mind purports to the heavens of thoughts and realms of ideas.

6- Do not be afraid of life, live it wisely.

7- My little princess, do your best to read books.. read many books and focous on those books that you find them full of imagination and adventure.

8- Read many books.. many good books. Read the books of George Eliot, Emily Brontë , Ernest Hemingway, Charles Dickens, Dostoevsky, Victor Hugo, Voltaire, Goethe and Marquez. Read the books of Western literature because they expend your imagination, relax your mind and illuminate the depth of your heart. Read for Nagib Mahfouz, Taha Hussein, Mansour al-Hakim, Al-Rifai and Manfaluti. Do not read for Ahlam Mastaganmi because of she has built her success on the sorrows of single women. Do not read for Nawal Alsadawi until you have your own independent character. Read about doubt before you read about certainty. There is no certainty if you have not passed the doubt. My advice for you my girl.. keep reading books..

9- Keep your secrets as secrets.. Keep them in the depth of your heart. Never trust a man before marriage.

10- It is your destiny my little angel to such a close minded society. A society that destroy the success of its individuals and seek to force its domination upon them and do whatever it could be done to cause them the failure. Never be disappointed if anybody attack you. Whenever you hear them talk about you from your back, be sure you are in the right path because only full spikes are thrown with stones.

11- If an eastern man fall in your love, he would do his best to conquer your kingdom and be the king of everything you have. He will consider you as being his one of his possessions. He will take everything from you, the past, present and future. He will make his best to make your soul a portrait of his soul. At that time, try to keep something special about you.

12- You are unique my little queen. You have something unique that no other body possess. We, human beings, have something unique that distinguishes each and everybody of us. Never imitate anybody nor be similar to anyone.

13- You are my daughter.. you are my queen. One day, you would be the queen of somebody else. Please do your best to please him.

14- Live your life intellectually. Think of each and every step before you pass it. Think of every word before you pronounce it.

15- Have your own mark in life. Do something for humanity. Never be on the fringe of civilization.

16- You are a female. You are the beauty and tranquility.. you are the happiness and greatness. You are a candle.. do not be anything else.

17- Never accept anything that contradict your mentality and the way you think and act according to. Your mind is your ultimate weapon and it is the ultimate standard that measures everything you have.

18- Never agrees upon anything unless you are convinced about. Never accept any decisions except the ones that were really yours.

19- Never let anybody make any decision on behave of you, whatever your relationship with this person, whether he is your father or mother or friend or husband or any other body. It is *your* decision my daughter and not the decision of any other body.

20- Always have the courage to say *NO* say that word at the accurate time and place. Say it to all people. Never be ashamed or shy of refusing anybody or anything. Say *NO* to me whenever you feel that I am standing as a barrier in your life.

21- It has never been wrong to fall in love with somebody. Be wise to learn from the mistakes of your love. Do not pay any attention to the Nizar Qabbani's poems about love and rebellion, betrayal and courage.. they are much ado about nothing.. never confess your love to any man before he do that never confess your feelings before he proves the sincerity of his feelings. Ask for the to prove his emotions towards you. Whenever he do that, be his heart and mind and soul.

22- My little angel.. I am your friend whenever you fall in love, tell me about that, so that I am going to provide you with my advices. Never be afraid of me my babe.

23- Try to make the sound of reason higher that the sound of the heart. I have said *try* because of I know that sometimes, it is so difficult to control our feelings and emotions.

24- You are a female. You voice is so quiet. The sound of mind is higher than the sound of heart. You are usually shy. Never raise your voice to prove any idea. Never swear. Never laugh loudly in front of people. Never try to be distinguished by acting in a different way from the community. Be successful. Be a true female.

25- Machiavelli says, "the end justifies the means" and there is an international axiom says, "everything is fair in love and war," my baby We are human beings. Never let your destination to reach the top of glory let you forget your principles and dogmas. Think of achieving your dreams following the legal methods. Fight for your goal till the last moment. Never give up till you reach your goal. Follow the path of truth.

26- Never follow a devious ways.

27- Cheat nobody. Nobody refuse the bad actions for himself and accept them for the others. Do not take a married man from his wife.

28- Be vigilant of your free time my girl.. it is your bitter enemy. Try to fill your free time with a hobby or an activity.

29- Write your own diaries.. write your dreams and plans.. write your hopes and wishes.. write whatever you like to write and have your own secrets.. write poetry or prose, stories or dialogues. If you wish, learn how to draw or how to play music. One day, you will fell with an extraordinary energy and you would think of the best way and the most secured way to have use of it and at that time, if you would not have a hobby or a job that you like, boredom will be your own kingdom and sadness would be all your realms. Your internal soul would weakened and your energy would fade away and your heart would beat in a different way. Reading is a beautiful story my girl, as for writing, it is another great story.

30- Have a goal in your life that you seek its achieve. Never be shy or ashamed of your goals.

31- There is an exception for every role and even the role of exception has it is own exception. Never worry for those who are trying to let you down my girl. Never care about the laughs of the elderly women. Be the exception for their role my baby. Never care for what they do. Never care for what they say. Your success is their failure and your failure is their success. Never care for anything. Go on in your way and be the pain in their nick.

32- The community is corrupted my girl. Try to coexistence with that. I have said *coexistence* and not accept.

33- Do not care about the fashion, la mode and clothes. Only empty minded people think of them. Try to transcendence my girl.

34- I will not ask you to have a role model in your life, nor would I ask you to follow anybody. Whenever you grow up and have your own mentality, you may have that role model.

35- Beware of vanity my girl and be humble in your life. How much wise, knowledge or beauty you reach in your life, never think of looking at anybody in a haughty way. Be humble my girl. The greatness of any female in her being humble. Be a great creature in the life of others and never forget the words of Togre, *"the more we become humble, we approach the greatness."*

36- Breathe slowly and think slowly. Never go to bed before you prepare your goals and dreams for the next day. If you have any idea, write it down. Never depend on your own memory because memory is not stable. Never underestimate any idea how much small it seems to be. *Ideas are sacred, never forget that!*

37- My small girl.. since the moment you were a very small an embryo in , I used to play the great music of Andre Rieu, Yanni and Mozart for you. You grow up in an atmosphere related to knowledge and books, information and translation. Since you were 15 months old, you used to take my papers and books and then you imitate what I was doing! And full pages with great and lovely signs and lines and laugh when I was looking at you! I hope that this period in your life has its own influence upon your character when you grow up.

38- Never be distinguished nor make yourself distinguished by your clothes. Be unique with your heart, mind and soul. Never let anybody fall in your love due to the clothes you wear. Let him adore your heart and mind, not your external skin.

39- I am sure that you know the ten commandments. Stick to them my girl.

40- Do not ask anybody to imitate something you are doing, or something you like to do. Each one has its own unique characteristics.

41- Do not try to escape your reality by resorting to bed or resorting to eat. Never kill your time by sleeping. Have only the amount you need.

42- As for any woman, the wisdom is in the mind, in the ideas she thinks about, in her looks at those who are around her, in her tranquil, in her calmness. That is the true wisdom my girl.

43- Do not seduce anybody. Be very normal in your own acts and actions.

44- We always have our decisions to have in our life. Live your life wisely. Do not harsh in deciding your own fatal decisions. Calm down when you think of the important decision. Sometimes, follow the advice of Helen Keller when she said, *"Life Is Either a Daring Adventure or Nothing."*

45- When you grow up and get married and have children, choose the names of your children before their coming.

Try to get used of their existence before their coming. Never force your opinion.

46- Never be weak, be smart. Being smart and strong are not contradicted. Be flexible like the filled spike of wheat.. it does not care about the wind, how much strong was it, it stand humbly full of wise and intelligence.

47- Many people will tell you that you are so beautiful and will praise and flatter the Beauty of your body and your clothes. Very few will praise the greatness of your mind and mentality. My girl, at that time, choose the fittest and most appropriate and the most receptive and flexible.

48- If a rich man, an intelligence man, and man of knowledge try to give you their surname, try to choose one of them, and then pour the characteristics of the two other men upon him. Be aware of haste. Be wise when you have important decisions.

49- After you marry that man you have chosen, try to be his soul mate. Tell him stories, speak about tales and novels. Tell him about princes and princesses, about heroes and knights, about Aladdin and Ali Baba, about Balqis and Solomon, about Scheherazade and Shahriyar. Let him get used of telling him a story every night. Change the mentality of your husband and make him a great man in front of the others. Change his mentality and personality. Let him sink down to the depth in the charm of your eyes.

50- It has never be wrong to commit a mistake. Learn from your mistakes so that you never do them again.

51- Respect your appointments. Respect your own words. Do not rebuke or criticize or advice or counsel anybody in front of the others. The advice in secret and the scandal in public. Respect people.. respect yourself.

52- You are a priceless gem. Accept this truth and let others accept it. Whenever you are a lovely respectable person, they will all admit that you are unique.

53- Do not care if you notices that the people who are having the same mentality you have are few. Your way is difficult but the end is always fruitful.

54- Never seek your goals before the appropriate time. The sin of Adam and Eve was not that they had eaten the forbidden fruit rather than was that they had eaten the fruit before its appropriate time.

55- Do not be angry my little angel. The first thing you are going to lose when you become angry is your femininity. Whenever you lose it, nothing is going to bring it back.

56- If poverty was a man, I would have killed him. Poverty is not only related to money.. it is the poverty of conscience and awareness.. poverty of heart and soul. My girl, be the warrior who is going to kill any state of poverty. Never be ashamed if you spent your life as a poor girl. I have provided you with the mentality that will help you not to be poor in your life.

57- Never depend on generalization in your life because of everything is relative. Freedom, slavery, love and hate, pessimism and optimism, they are all relative dogmas exactly like angels and demons. The guardian angel who is defending and protecting you and frightening your enemy is a bitter demon for your enemy.

58- Life is a journey.. life is an adventure. Let your journey be fascinating and never give up. Have your own challenges and own adventure. Live your journey and enjoy your life.

59- Whether you accepted or refuse any of the commandments, it is always your choice. My role is just to refine the road of the journey for you my girl and you would be the one who will have that journey. I am the supporter my girl and not the dominator.

60- My girl, never accept the injustice because of you are afraid of the community. Never accept the scandal for the fear of the community. Never let your silence be the fuel that burn other victims. Be the candle that ignite itself in order to illuminate the others.

61- Do not make me nor your mother the standard of your success or failure. Be the observer and not the observed. Never be afraid of the truth, if one day I stood against you and you had a goal at that time, you have full privilege to refuse my orders. My role was just and only to give you advice, and it would be my role for the rest of my life.

62- Do not pay any attention to the words of your mother whenever they are against the best of you. One day, Aristotle was asked about Plato and he said, *I love my teacher but love the truth more than him*. The ultimate goodness is the truth my girl, and the supreme reality is the truthiness. I know that my words are still so difficult for you to conceive but one day, you would understand them my girl.

63- Trust your instincts. Have your own dreams. Never tell your dream to anybody. People used to let down the dreams regardless how great and supreme they were. Never tell your dream to anybody. Keep it in the depth of your heart. Never be afraid of the great dreams, Almighty God created great dreams for great people.

64- The foolish does not forgive nor forget, the naïve forgive and forget and the wise forgive but never forget. Be wise my girl, it is my ultimate advice for you.

65- All materials decay.. the chair, table, house, tree, earth, universe, and life.. everything is going to decay and be nothing. The physical existence is going to decay and the immortality is for the mind my little queen.

66- Be charm babe, do not be simple, do not be naïve.

67- Never disclose your secrets to anybody.

68- Do not limit yourself. Never have any limit for your ambition, nor have any bonds for your mind .. the greatest question was *what if?* So do not limit yourself. Never apply the model of anybody upon you.

69- Knowledge and culture, moderation and civilization are all general conceptions that are not centralized in the university. University is only points to the way you are supposed to follow.. it is not that way by itself. The university would never be an alternative for seeking the truth by yourself. I will never force you to have a university study unless you like to have it. Let life be your own university and the universe is your own laboratory.

70- Never lose your self-confidence in front of anybody. Never do concessions under any situation. Never limit or lower your requirements in order to satisfy anybody. You know your *own* dream more than any other person.

71- Your body is a sacred kingdom. Protect it as much as you can. It is the deposit of God. Keep it and protect it.

72- Sometimes, it is great to act in a childish way in your life. It is also great to be naughty and act carelessly at some situations. Remember my girl, do that at the appropriate time and place, in front of the suitable person.

73- It is not important to be successful cooker. The shortest way to the heart of man is to understand him and understand his desires and emotions.. it is to respect him and adore what he is doing for you.. for the naïve, the shortest way for the heart of man is his stomach. You are not naïve my girl.

74- Never be simple minded. Always be cleaver and act in a clever way in your life.

75- Let your *no* be *maybe* and your *maybe* is *yes* and never say *no* in your life.

76- At least, learn one foreign language.

77- Never build your happiness on the disasters of the others. Never build your castle on the ruins of the others.

78- Nothing is stable my girl.. everything is changing.

79- Have your own moments.. have your own sacred time. As for me, reading a classic book in front of the fireplace in a heavy shower night in winter is the best moment I can imagine to live. Have your own special time.

80- Have a library in your future house so that this library become the rabbit hole that can take you to other realms.

81- One of the most beautiful moments that you might face in your life is when you lie down on your back and look at the stars at clear night in September. Do that at least one time in your life.

82- I will keep calling you my child and my baby till the moment of your marriage. At that time, you would be the child and baby of another man.

83- Be like a book my girl. Be an open book for your friend and keep some closed pages for your love, some other pages for your husband, and some other pages for yourself. Keep some sentences for yourself that never disclose to anybody.

84- Never be cheap my girl. Do not give your body to anybody, for any purpose or goal. You are sacred my girl. Never concede anything for the sake of gaining something else. The first thing you are going to lose is yourself and there is no way to gain it back again.

85- Never complain about anything, in front of anybody until you trust him.

86- Never show your pains in front of your friend or your enemy. The first one will be sad and melancholy for you, while the second will be happy and gloated for you. If you trust your husband, share him your pains.

87- A Faithful woman is always satisfied to have one man to be her husband, friend, love and brother. As for men, they tend to have more than one woman in their life. Try to fulfill the depths of your husband.

88- Never interrupt somebody while he is talking and never understand somebody fast. Give all people enough time to clarify the ideas they are thinking about.

89- Be honest and explicit. Do not hide yourself and never hide your ideas.

90- Do not limit your ambition and goals with a certain stage that whenever you achieve it you stop everything. You might achieve your goals and dreams while you are still 35 years old. Never have a limit for your goals and dreams.

91- In love, jealousy is like water for a rose, little refreshes and too much destroys. Control your feelings and emotions.

92- My girl. Right now I am writing to you these words while you are still messing with my papers and looking at me while you are laughing and then go back to your absurdity. I pray God that one day you read my commandments deeply and understand their meanings.

93- My girl. I have never loved a girl like I have loved you. May God protect you my little angel.

94- My daughter, I will do my best to provide you with the best I can do in your life. One day, you are going to marry and have your own children. Deal with gently and with moderation.. deal with them in a civilized and urbane way of life.

95- My girl, one day, you are going to have your own viewpoint, and your own logic.. you are going to refuse many of my requests and provide me with convincing reasons for our refusal. That moment would be the greatest moment in my life.

96- Larin.. you are the queen, you are la Reine, you are associated with the laurel leaves. You are the secret and the sacred. You are the mystery and the vagueness, you are the amulet and the talisman, you are the alpha and omega, you are the wisdom and knowledge. My girl, deal with all people humbly and never be haughty.

97- My girl, we have read many books about the best way to deal with you. We have learnt how to bring you up before you were born. We have planned for your coming. My advice for you my little girl, plan for the future of your children before they were born.

98- My baby, I will not ask you to be like all fishes that swim with the tide, I will not ask you to be like the salmon fish that swim against the tide. Be flexible my girl. Swim against the tide when the waves are calm and quiet and swim with the tide whenever it is the time of the storms and tornados.

99- Walk under rain.. be rebellious against everything. Do not be afraid of having your clothes wet. Laugh on those who are accusing you of being lunatic.. they still live in the Middle Ages.

100- Larin.. Be the phoenix that never dies. Never lose hope whatever the obstacles are great.

101- Do not be afraid of Truth, and never be afraid of saying the truth or passing the path of the justice even if the number of those who follow that way are few. Whatever this road become long and thorny, you would find the lifeline at its end.

102- Never show respect to anybody by kissing his hand whatever is the goal or the reason. Do not bow for anybody. Never kiss my hand or the hand of your mother as showing us respect and love, obedience or satisfaction. I so much hate this act my little angel. Never be subordinate to anybody my girl.

103- Be yourself, and never subordinate to anybody. Have your *own* independent character and never be under the objection of anyone.

104- Forget everything connected with liberation of women.. forget all slogans and mottos that calls for preserving and defending of the women. They are all banal slogans. Have in your mind subliminal goals and plans like liberation of human being in general and liberation of his mind and his thought from fear, anxiety and doubt. You have a great message and your message is dictated to the whole humanity and not to women away from the others. Never be simple minded to follow such trifle mottos.

105- Whenever you have the chance to travel, do that without hesitation. If you could not have the chance to travel, then let your mind purports to the heavens of thoughts and realms of ideas.

106- Do not be afraid of life, live it wisely.

107- My little princess, do your best to read books.. read many books and focous on those books that you find them full of imagination and adventure.

108- Read many books.. many good books. Read the books of George Eliot, Emily Brontë , Ernest Hemingway, Charles Dickens, Dostoevsky, Victor Hugo, Voltaire, Goethe and Marquez. Read the books of Western literature because they expend your imagination, relax your mind and illuminate the depth of your heart. Read for Nagib Mahfouz, Taha Hussein, Mansour al-Hakim, Al-Rifai and Manfaluti. Do not read for Ahlam Mastaganmi because of she has built her success on the sorrows of single women. Do not read for Nawal Alsadawi until you have your own independent character. Read about doubt before you read about certainty. There is no certainty if you have not passed the doubt. My advice for you my girl.. keep reading books..

109- Keep your secrets as secrets.. Keep them in the depth of your heart. Never trust a man before marriage.

110- It is your destiny my little angel to such a close minded society. A society that destroy the success of its individuals and seek to force its domination upon them and do whatever it could be done to cause them the failure. Never be disappointed if anybody attack you. Whenever you hear them talk about you from your back, be sure you are in the right path because only full spikes are thrown with stones.

111- If an eastern man fall in your love, he would do his best to conquer your kingdom and be the king of everything you have. He will consider you as being his one of his possessions. He will take everything from you, the past, present and future. He will make his best to make your soul a portrait of his soul. At that time, try to keep something special about you.

112- You are unique my little queen. You have something unique that no other body possess. We, human beings, have something unique that distinguishes each and everybody of us. Never imitate anybody nor be similar to anyone.

113- You are my daughter.. you are my queen. One day, you would be the queen of somebody else. Please do your best to please him.

114- Live your life intellectually. Think of each and every step before you pass it. Think of every word before you pronounce it.

115- Have your own mark in life. Do something for humanity. Never be on the fringe of civilization.

116- You are a female. You are the beauty and tranquility.. you are the happiness and greatness. You are a candle.. do not be anything else.

117- Never accept anything that contradict your mentality and the way you think and act according to. Your mind is your ultimate weapon and it is the ultimate standard that measures everything you have.

118- Never agrees upon anything unless you are convinced about. Never accept any decisions except the ones that were really yours.

119- Never let anybody make any decision on behave of you, whatever your relationship with this person, whether he is your father or mother or friend or husband or any other body. It is *your* decision my daughter and not the decision of any other body.

120- Always have the courage to say *NO* say that word at the accurate time and place. Say it to all people. Never be ashamed or shy of refusing anybody or anything. Say *NO* to me whenever you feel that I am standing as a barrier in your life.

121- It has never been wrong to fall in love with somebody. Be wise to learn from the mistakes of your love. Do not pay any attention to the Nizar Qabbani's poems about love and rebellion, betrayal and courage.. they are much ado about nothing.. never confess your love to any man before he do that never confess your feelings before he proves the sincerity of his feelings. Ask for the to prove his emotions towards you. Whenever he do that, be his heart and mind and soul.

122- My little angel.. I am your friend whenever you fall in love, tell me about that, so that I am going to provide you with my advices. Never be afraid of me my babe.

123- Try to make the sound of reason higher that the sound of the heart. I have said *try* because of I know that sometimes, it is so difficult to control our feelings and emotions.

124- You are a female. You voice is so quiet. The sound of mind is higher than the sound of heart. You are usually shy. Never raise your voice to prove any idea. Never swear. Never laugh loudly in front of people. Never try to be distinguished by acting in a different way from the community. Be successful. Be a true female.

125- Machiavelli says, "the end justifies the means" and there is an international axiom says, "everything is fair in love and war," my baby We are human beings. Never let your destination to reach the top of glory let you forget your principles and dogmas. Think of achieving your dreams following the legal methods. Fight for your goal till the last moment. Never give up till you reach your goal. Follow the path of truth.

126- Never follow a devious ways.

127- Cheat nobody. Nobody refuse the bad actions for himself and accept them for the others. Do not take a married man from his wife.

128- Be vigilant of your free time my girl.. it is your bitter enemy. Try to fill your free time with a hobby or an activity.

129- Write your own diaries.. write your dreams and plans.. write your hopes and wishes.. write whatever you like to write and have your own secrets.. write poetry or prose, stories or dialogues. If you wish, learn how to draw or how to play music. One day, you will fell with an extraordinary energy and you would think of the best way and the most secured way to have use of it and at that time, if you would not have a hobby or a job that you like, boredom will be your own kingdom and sadness would be all your realms. Your internal soul would weakened and your energy would fade away and your heart would beat in a different way. Reading is a beautiful story my girl, as for writing, it is another great story.

130- Have a goal in your life that you seek its achieve. Never be shy or ashamed of your goals.

131- There is an exception for every role and even the role of exception has it is own exception. Never worry for those who are trying to let you down my girl. Never care about the laughs of the elderly women. Be the exception for their role my baby. Never care for what they do. Never care for what they say. Your success is their failure and your failure is their success. Never care for anything. Go on in your way and be the pain in their nick.

132- The community is corrupted my girl. Try to coexistence with that. I have said *coexistence* and not accept.

133- Do not care about the fashion, la mode and clothes. Only empty minded people think of them. Try to transcendence my girl.

134- I will not ask you to have a role model in your life, nor would I ask you to follow anybody. Whenever you grow up and have your own mentality, you may have that role model.

135- Beware of vanity my girl and be humble in your life. How much wise, knowledge or beauty you reach in your life, never think of looking at anybody in a haughty way. Be humble my girl. The greatness of any female in her being humble. Be a great creature in the life of others and never forget the words of Togre, *"the more we become humble, we approach the greatness."*

136- Breathe slowly and think slowly. Never go to bed before you prepare your goals and dreams for the next day. If you have any idea, write it down. Never depend on your own memory because memory is not stable. Never underestimate any idea how much small it seems to be. *Ideas are sacred, never forget that!*

137- My small girl.. since the moment you were a very small an embryo in , I used to play the great music of Andre Rieu, Yanni and Mozart for you. You grow up in an atmosphere related to knowledge and books, information and translation. Since you were 15 months old, you used to take my papers and books and then you imitate what I was doing! And full pages with great and lovely signs and lines and laugh when I was looking at you! I hope that this period in your life has its own influence upon your character when you grow up.

138- Never be distinguished nor make yourself distinguished by your clothes. Be unique with your heart, mind and soul. Never let anybody fall in your love due to the clothes you wear. Let him adore your heart and mind, not your external skin.

139- I am sure that you know the ten commandments. Stick to them my girl.

140- Do not ask anybody to imitate something you are doing, or something you like to do. Each one has its own unique characteristics.

141- Do not try to escape your reality by resorting to bed or resorting to eat. Never kill your time by sleeping. Have only the amount you need.

142- As for any woman, the wisdom is in the mind, in the ideas she thinks about, in her looks at those who are around her, in her tranquil, in her calmness. That is the true wisdom my girl.

143- Do not seduce anybody. Be very normal in your own acts and actions.

144- We always have our decisions to have in our life. Live your life wisely. Do not harsh in deciding your own fatal decisions. Calm down when you think of the important decision. Sometimes, follow the advice of Helen Keller when she said, *"Life Is Either a Daring Adventure or Nothing."*

145- When you grow up and get married and have children, choose the names of your children before their coming. Try to get used of their existence before their coming. Never force your opinion.

146- Never be weak, be smart. Being smart and strong are not contradicted. Be flexible like the filled spike of wheat.. it does not care about the wind, how much strong was it, it stand humbly full of wise and intelligence.

147- Many people will tell you that you are so beautiful and will praise and flatter the Beauty of your body and your clothes. Very few will praise the greatness of your mind and mentality. My girl, at that time, choose the fittest and most appropriate and the most receptive and flexible.

148- If a rich man, an intelligence man, and man of knowledge try to give you their surname, try to choose one of them, and then pour the characteristics of the two other men upon him. Be aware of haste. Be wise when you have important decisions.

149- After you marry that man you have chosen, try to be his soul mate. Tell him stories, speak about tales and novels. Tell him about princes and princesses, about heroes and knights, about Aladdin and Ali Baba, about Balqis and Solomon, about Scheherazade and Shahriyar. Let him get used of telling him a story every night. Change the mentality of your husband and make him a great man in front of the others. Change his mentality and personality. Let him sink down to the depth in the charm of your eyes.

150- It has never be wrong to commit a mistake. Learn from your mistakes so that you never do them again.

151- Respect your appointments. Respect your own words. Do not rebuke or criticize or advice or counsel anybody in front of the others. The advice in secret and the scandal in public. Respect people.. respect yourself.

152- You are a priceless gem. Accept this truth and let others accept it. Whenever you are a lovely respectable person, they will all admit that you are unique.

153- Do not care if you notices that the people who are having the same mentality you have are few. Your way is difficult but the end is always fruitful.

154- Never seek your goals before the appropriate time. The sin of Adam and Eve was not that they had eaten the forbidden fruit rather than was that they had eaten the fruit before its appropriate time.

155- Do not be angry my little angel. The first thing you are going to lose when you become angry is your femininity. Whenever you lose it, nothing is going to bring it back.

156- If poverty was a man, I would have killed him. Poverty is not only related to money.. it is the poverty of conscience and awareness.. poverty of heart and soul. My girl, be the warrior who is going to kill any state of poverty. Never be ashamed if you spent your life as a poor girl. I have provided you with the mentality that will help you not to be poor in your life.

157- Never depend on generalization in your life because of everything is relative. Freedom, slavery, love and hate, pessimism and optimism, they are all relative dogmas exactly like angels and demons. The guardian angel who is defending and protecting you and frightening your enemy is a bitter demon for your enemy.

158- Life is a journey.. life is an adventure. Let your journey be fascinating and never give up. Have your own challenges and own adventure. Live your journey and enjoy your life.

159- Whether you accepted or refuse any of the commandments, it is always your choice. My role is just to refine the road of the journey for you my girl and you would be the one who will have that journey. I am the supporter my girl and not the dominator.

160- My girl, never accept the injustice because of you are afraid of the community. Never accept the scandal for the fear of the community. Never let your silence be the fuel that burn other victims. Be the candle that ignite itself in order to illuminate the others.

161- Do not make me nor your mother the standard of your success or failure. Be the observer and not the observed. Never be afraid of the truth, if one day I stood against you and you had a goal at that time, you have full privilege to refuse my orders. My role was just and only to give you advice, and it would be my role for the rest of my life.

162- Do not pay any attention to the words of your mother whenever they are against the best of you. One day, Aristotle was asked about Plato and he said, *I love my teacher but love the truth more than him*. The ultimate goodness is the truth my girl, and the supreme reality is the truthiness. I know that my words are still so difficult for you to conceive but one day, you would understand them my girl.

163- Trust your instincts. Have your own dreams. Never tell your dream to anybody. People used to let down the dreams regardless how great and supreme they were. Never tell your dream to anybody. Keep it in the depth of your heart. Never be afraid of the great dreams, Almighty God created great dreams for great people.

164- The foolish does not forgive nor forget, the naïve forgive and forget and the wise forgive but never forget. Be wise my girl, it is my ultimate advice for you.

165- All materials decay.. the chair, table, house, tree, earth, universe, and life.. everything is going to decay and be nothing. The physical existence is going to decay and the immortality is for the mind my little queen.

166- Be charm babe, do not be simple, do not be naïve.

167- Never disclose your secrets to anybody.

168- Do not limit yourself. Never have any limit for your ambition, nor have any bonds for your mind .. the greatest question was *what if?* So do not limit yourself. Never apply the model of anybody upon you.

169- Knowledge and culture, moderation and civilization are all general conceptions that are not centralized in the university. University is only points to the way you are supposed to follow.. it is not that way by itself. The university would never be an alternative for seeking the truth by yourself. I will never force you to have a university study unless you like to have it. Let life be your own university and the universe is your own laboratory.

170- Never lose your self-confidence in front of anybody. Never do concessions under any situation. Never limit or lower your requirements in order to satisfy anybody. You know your *own* dream more than any other person.

171- Your body is a sacred kingdom. Protect it as much as you can. It is the deposit of God. Keep it and protect it.

172- Sometimes, it is great to act in a childish way in your life. It is also great to be naughty and act carelessly at some situations. Remember my girl, do that at the appropriate time and place, in front of the suitable person.

173- It is not important to be successful cooker. The shortest way to the heart of man is to understand him and understand his desires and emotions.. it is to respect him and adore what he is doing for you.. for the naïve, the shortest way for the heart of man is his stomach. You are not naïve my girl.

174- Never be simple minded. Always be cleaver and act in a clever way in your life.

175- Let your *no* be *maybe* and your *maybe* is *yes* and never say *no* in your life.

176- At least, learn one foreign language.

177- Never build your happiness on the disasters of the others. Never build your castle on the ruins of the others.

178- Nothing is stable my girl.. everything is changing.

179- Have your own moments.. have your own sacred time. As for me, reading a classic book in front of the fireplace in a heavy shower night in winter is the best moment I can imagine to live. Have your own special time.

180- Have a library in your future house so that this library become the rabbit hole that can take you to other realms.

181- One of the most beautiful moments that you might face in your life is when you lie down on your back and look at the stars at clear night in September. Do that at least one time in your life.

182- I will keep calling you my child and my baby till the moment of your marriage. At that time, you would be the child and baby of another man.

183- Be like a book my girl. Be an open book for your friend and keep some closed pages for your love, some other pages for your husband, and some other pages for yourself. Keep some sentences for yourself that never disclose to anybody.

184- Never be cheap my girl. Do not give your body to anybody, for any purpose or goal. You are sacred my girl. Never concede anything for the sake of gaining something else. The first thing you are going to lose is yourself and there is no way to gain it back again.

185- Never complain about anything, in front of anybody until you trust him.

186- Never show your pains in front of your friend or your enemy. The first one will be sad and melancholy for you, while the second will be happy and gloated for you. If you trust your husband, share him your pains.

187- A Faithful woman is always satisfied to have one man to be her husband, friend, love and brother. As for men, they tend to have more than one woman in their life. Try to fulfill the depths of your husband.

188- Never interrupt somebody while he is talking and never understand somebody fast. Give all people enough time to clarify the ideas they are thinking about.

189- Be honest and explicit. Do not hide yourself and never hide your ideas.

190- Do not limit your ambition and goals with a certain stage that whenever you achieve it you stop everything. You might achieve your goals and dreams while you are still 35 years old. Never have a limit for your goals and dreams.

191- In love, jealousy is like water for a rose, little refreshes and too much destroys. Control your feelings and emotions.

192- My girl. Right now I am writing to you these words while you are still messing with my papers and looking at me while you are laughing and then go back to your absurdity. I pray God that one day you read my commandments deeply and understand their meanings.

193- My girl. I have never loved a girl like I have loved you. May God protect you my little angel.

194- My daughter, I will do my best to provide you with the best I can do in your life. One day, you are going to marry and have your own children. Deal with gently and with moderation.. deal with them in a civilized and urbane way of life.

195- My girl, one day, you are going to have your own viewpoint, and your own logic.. you are going to refuse many of my requests and provide me with convincing reasons for our refusal. That moment would be the greatest moment in my life.

196- Larin.. you are the queen, you are la Reine, you are associated with the laurel leaves. You are the secret and the sacred. You are the mystery and the vagueness, you are the amulet and the talisman, you are the alpha and omega, you are the wisdom and knowledge. My girl, deal with all people humbly and never be haughty.

197- My girl, we have read many books about the best way to deal with you. We have learnt how to bring you up before you were born. We have planned for your coming. My advice for you my little girl, plan for the future of your children before they were born.

198- My baby, I will not ask you to be like all fishes that swim with the tide, I will not ask you to be like the salmon fish that swim against the tide. Be flexible my girl. Swim against the tide when the waves are calm and quiet and swim with the tide whenever it is the time of the storms and tornados.

199- Walk under rain.. be rebellious against everything. Do not be afraid of having your clothes wet. Laugh on those who are accusing you of being lunatic.. they still live in the Middle Ages.

200- Larin.. Be the phoenix that never dies. Never lose hope whatever the obstacles are great.

To my girl Larin.

Be the dream my little angel. Follow your dream in order to achieve your goal and be careless about those behind you. Do not be afraid of their laughs. Make these laughs your motivations towards success. Never give up my girl. You will achieve your goal.

A.I.
ARTIFICIAL INTELLIGENCE

أكثر ذكاءً منا
صعود ذكاء الآلات

تأليف : ستيوارت آرمسترونغ

ترجمة : مصطفى كيالي

همسات سريالية

نصوص وقضايا وجودية

مصطفى كيالي

إعَاقَةُ التَّعلُّم

متلازمة عسر القراءة و الصعوبات المرافقة لها

مصطفى كيالي

نَظَريات التَّعلُّم

Learning Theories

إعداد وترجمة: مصطفى كيالي

SURREAL
WHISPERS

ARABIC EDITION

MUSTAFA KAYYALI

You may contact with the writer on the following:

Email: alchemical.studies@gmail.com

Facebook: www.facebook.com/moustafa.kayyali

LinkedIn: www.sy.linkedin.com/in/mustafa-kayyali-6ba09298

www.goodreads.com/author/show/15217017.Mustafa_Kayyali

www. kbuuk.com/kb/mustafakayyali

www.flipsnack.com/es/Mustafakayyali/

www.smashwords.com/profile/view/MustafaKayyli

www.proz.com/profile/1962536

www.translatorscafe.com/cafe/member290568.htm

www.scribd.com/author/324965725/Mustafa-Kayyali

www.people.bayt.com/mustafa-kayyali-22590798

www.bol.com/nl/c/algemeen/mustafa-kayyali/

www.lulu.com/shop/mustafa-kayyali

www.issuu.com/moustafakayyali

Mobile: +963 933 877 869

Google: Mustafa Kayyali